Xiaoyaoshuai

Wuji System Free Fighting Take Down Routine

By

Shou-Yu Liang

&

Wen-Ching Wu

Edited by

Denise Breiter-Wu

The Way of the Dragon Publishing, Rhode Island, U.S.A.

Published by:

魟 The Way of the Dragon Publishing

P. O. Box 14561

East Providence, RI 02914-0561

United States of America

First Printing 2000

First Edition

Printed in the United States of America

9 8 7 6 5 4 3 2 1

Publisher's Cataloging-in-Publication Data

Wu, Wen-Ching, 1964-

 Xiaoyaoshuai: wuji system free fighting take down routine /
by Wen-Ching Wu and Shou-Yu Liang

 illus. p. cm.

 Includes bibliographical references and index

 ISBN 1-889659-12-6

 1. Martial arts--China. 2. Wrestling--China. 3. Kung fu. 4. Kung
fu--Wrestling. 5. Exercise. 6. Physical fitness. I. Liang, Shou-Yu. II.
Title.

796.812 5   99-76888

Table of Contents

Dedication

To my wife, Xiang-Yong: All my progress and advancement are inseparable from her hard work and dedication in maintaining the health and harmony of my family.

To my daughters, Helen and Maria; and to all my students and friends.

這本書獻給我的夫人，向勇女士。我的一切進步和成就都是與他辛勤勞動，維持健康的家庭分不開的。

獻給我的女兒，梁好和梁爽和我所有的學生和朋友們。

Shou-Yu Liang

梁守渝

Fall 1999

Warning-Disclaimer

The exercises in this book may be too mentally and physically demanding for some people. Readers should use their own discretion and consult their doctor before engaging in these exercises. The authors and the publisher shall have neither liability nor responsibility to any person or entity with respect to any loss or damage caused, or alleged to be caused, directly or indirectly by reading or following the instructions in this book.

Acknowledgments

Thanks to Sanford Lee (李相燁) and Sam Carroll for assisting in the demonstration of the techniques; thanks to Frank Whitsitt-Lynch for proof reading the manuscript; and thanks to Sarah Alexander for preparing the Publisher's Cataloging in Publication.

Preface by:

Shou-Yu Liang

Chinese Wushu (martial arts, 武術) is very deep and profound. Among the many components of Wushu, ti (踢), da (打), shuai (摔), na (拿), and tuishou (push hands, 推手) skills are essential to learn to be a complete martial artist. In this book, we have focused on the shuai (short for shuaijiao) skill. Shuai skill is a very important part of free fighting skills. In sanshou competitions, shuaijiao techniques are commonly used by the champion competitors. Competitors in free Taiji Push Hands (太極推手) and Bagua Sanshou (八卦散手) also rely heavily on shuaijiao skills to gain victory. In an actual fight, the opportunity to use shuaijiao skills are even greater.

If a Chinese martial artists is not well versed in shuaijiao, his/her martial ability is not considered to be complete. Sometimes, a strong individual with little or no martial arts experience can hold on to a martial artist without shuaijiao skill and he/she will have a difficult time escaping the hold.

There is a popular saying in Wushu, "Masters refrain from people that simply grab a hold of you like they are falling off a 100 story high rise, and won't let go."

In the Qing Dynasty (1644-1911 A.D.), one of the important areas of training for the royal bodyguards was shuaijiao skill; in addition to bare-handed, saber, spear, staff, and sword fighting techniques.

Martial artists that train shuaijiao regularly are physically strong and healthy, brave and skilled in fighting. Shuaijiao training can also solidify and further one's fighting abilities in other areas. Today, shuaijiao is also a very good sport activity.

Shuaijiao is not a style or system. All styles of Wushu have their own shuaijiao techniques. I have loved shuaijiao since I was a child, and have competed in many shuaijiao competitions. My shuaijiao experience has assisted me significantly in my advancement in the other components of my Wushu training. In recent years, I have written two books relating to shuaijiao. One covers Sanshou Kuaijioa (Chinese Fast Wrestling for Fighting), and another covers traditional shuaijiao techniques, to be published shortly. Hopefully, these books will assist in your training.

There are several hundred traditional shuaijiao techniques. It is very difficult to remember all of them. When there is not a partner to practice with, it is even more difficult to remember all the techniques.

The shuaijiao routine presented in this book can help participants remember the most basic and effective shuaijiao techniques. The name of this routine is "Wuji Xiaoyaoshuai". It is composed of 36 of the most important shuaijiao techniques linked together and practiced with Internal Style characteristics. It is designed to help participants remember and master the essential and important shuaijiao techniques.

When performed, the routine is graceful, yet dynamic, open and relaxing, gliding from one move to the next, giving participants more enjoyment while training effective shuaijiao techniques.

For many years, I have performed in many U.S., Canadian, and other international competitions, and have received great reception from my friends and colleagues. They have encouraged me to publish other routines in this series, including Xiaoyaona (qinna), Xiaoyaoquan (fist), Xiaoyaozhang (palm), Xiaoyaoguaitui (kicks). With the help and encouragement of my protégé, Wen-Ching Wu, this book is now ready to meet the general public.

Wuji implies limitlessness. In the technical movements, it implies many variations by analogy. That is, from the 36 techniques as a foundation, you have the option to vary them into numerous other techniques and combinations of techniques.

Xiaoyao implies, practice the movements with any characteristic you wish. You may use slower paced body movements backed with internal strength, or swift paced body movements with fajin, to completely express your personal characteristic.

Wen-Ching has coauthored several books with me. He has done a tremendous amount of work. I would like to take this opportunity to thank him. Also, thanks to his wife, Denise Breiter-Wu for her exact editing; and to The Way of the Dragon School instructors, Sam Carroll and Sanford Lee for assisting in the demonstration of the techniques.

Shou-Yu Liang

August 1999

無極逍遙摔

前 言

　　中國武術博大精深。其中的踢，打，摔，拿，推手等爲學武者必須鑽研的功夫。在這本書中我們主要介紹"摔法"。摔法在武術技擊中佔很重要的地位。在散手比賽中常用摔法。在太極自由推手和八卦散手中沒有摔法也很難取勝。在眞正的搏擊拼打中摔的機會更多。所以，如果不懂得摔法，功夫就不全面。有時，甚至一個不精通武術而力氣很打的人緊緊抱住你，你也很難擺脱。有句俗話説："教師（練功夫的師傅）怕扭（死扭住你不放的人）"。中國清朝時代（1644-1911）保衛皇宮的侍衛隊，除練習拳術及刀，搶，棍，劍諸器之外，相撲（摔跤）也是最重要的訓練項目之一。常練摔跤的人身體健壯，臂力過人，勇敢善戰。摔跤訓練爲進一步練習各種技擊奠定堅實的基礎。摔跤也是一種很好的體育運動。

　　各種拳術中都有一定的摔法。只不過沒有系統的歸納在一起。我從小就喜歡摔跤。參加過多次比賽。摔跤的訓練對我武術技擊的提高有很大的幫助。近幾年來，我寫過兩本有關摔跤的英文書籍。一本是《散手快跤》（已出版）。一本是《中國傳統摔跤》。希望對愛好者有所幫助。但是中國的摔跤技術太多，幾百個技術動作，很難記憶。特別是在沒有對手的情況下，個練習，很容易忘記一些技術動作。

　　這套《無極逍遙摔》套路，就能幫助學者記住最基本而又最重要的摔法。《無極逍遙摔》是把36個最重要的摔法用内家拳的方式表示和演練出來。使學者能夠牢記這些基本的，重要的方法。套路演練大方，舒展，飄逸倍增練習者的興趣。多年來我曾在中國表演過，又在美國，加拿大和國際武術比賽中表演過多次。得到同道門的高度評價。鼓勵我把這套逍遙摔和另外幾套，如逍遙拿，逍遙拳，逍遙掌，逍遙怪腿寫成書。在我的學生吳文慶先生的推動和幫助下，使這套逍遙摔首先問世。

　　"無極"是無止盡。特別是技術動作，舉一反三，以這三十幾個基本動作爲基礎，可變化成無數的動作，以及組合。"逍遙"的意思是隨便你用什麼方法演練。用柔和

11

的內力，身法，緩慢的節奏演練或是用較快的身法，剛猛的發勁演練都可以。充分發輝你自己的風格。

吳文慶先生與我合作出版了好幾本書。他作了大量的工作，在此向他表示感謝。另外向協助出書的吳迪倪思 (Denise Breiter-Wu)，凱柔薩姆 (Sam Carroll)，和李相燁 (Sanford Lee) 至以謝意。

梁守渝
1999 年 8 月

Introduction

All traditional Wushu (武術) styles have their own routines, containing the style's particular focus. Long Fist (長拳) routines emphasize kicking abilities for striking their opponent from a distance and are characterized by rapid advancing and retreating movements. Southern Style (南拳) routines emphasize close range applications and are characterized by rapid, compact, and closed range strikes. Internal Style (內家拳) routines emphasize circular, yielding, adhering abilities for leading their opponents into a disadvantageous position. Within their routines there are also many shuaijiao (摔跤 or 摔角) and qinna (擒拿) techniques which are not as obvious as the kicks and punches.

In the training of practical fighting applications, all styles train, *ti* (踢), *da* (打), *shuai* (摔), *na* (拿). *Ti* is the use of the legs for kicking. *Da* is the use of the arms for striking. *Shuai* is the use of take down techniques. *Na* is the use of controlling techniques to immobilize the opponent. The relative emphasize on ti, da, shuai, and na, of course depends on the style's focus. (For detailed coverage on the different components of Wushu, please refer to the book, *Kung Fu Elements*, by the authors.)

Shuaijiao is not a Wushu style. It is a component of all Wushu styles. It has also been a popular competition event since ancient times. It was also know as jiaodi (角抵), jiaoli (角力), xianpu (相扑), etc. It's objective is to skillfully utilize the body's leverage to take down the opponent or distress the opponent. In free fighting applications, a more specific shuaijiao approach is used. It is called kuaishuai (快摔) or kuaijiao (快跤), meaning fast take down. In kuaishuai, the practitioner does not struggle with their opponents. Once they engage, the take down is accomplished right away. In the applications, kicking, hooking, locking, and tripping with the leg; striking, grabbing, and pushing with the arms; or leaning and striking with the upper body, are often combined to accomplish an effective and devastating take down.

The applications are generally accomplished with the use of the shoulders, elbows, hips, palms, and/or the knees as the pivot point to take down the opponent. With the proper use of the body's leverage, a practitioner is easily able to take down their opponent with a shrugging of the shoulders, a turning of the waist, a twisting of the hips, a dropping of the elbow, a dropping of the knee, or a hooking of the leg. The use of angles opposite to the normal movements of the joints and the use of leverage to off set the opponent's balance are also essential for a successful take down technique.

Unlike most shuaijiao only competitions, kuaijiao applications often include kicks and punches. In an offensive application, kuaijiao utilizes kicks and punches to set up a take down. If the opponent is able to neutralize the take down, then they kick or punch again, or do a qinna technique. After the take down, they continue to strike until the opponent is completely subdued. Kuaijiao can be used in both a defensive, as well as, in an offensive situation.

Combat readiness training traditionally consisted of training both specific techniques individually or as a routine; and with partners. It does not make any difference which Wushu style you choose to focus on. From understanding and the ability to apply sufficient techniques, you will be able to combine the techniques in different variations or vary the techniques, and be able to improvise during actual combat. The 36 take down techniques in this routine will give you a solid base for hundreds of different combinations and variations.

There is nothing new that can be created in terms of practical applications or movements in Wushu. Over the millenniums, all the effective and logical movements have been created. It would be a waste of time to create something that is already available. Even though there is nothing new that can be created in the field of Wushu, there is still room for improvement. In order for anything to improve, it is imperative that newer generations learn from the old and add on to information already available. Otherwise, the art will stagnate and eventually become extinct. The improvements in Wushu are in the redesign and reorganization of the old to come up with practical uses and effective training methods for today's martial artists.

By reorganizing what he learned along with decades of experience, Shou-Yu Liang has combined the essence of many Wushu styles and has come up with a series of routines to assist practitioners in attaining the essence of *ti, da, shuai*, and *na* more readily and efficiently. The Wuji Series of routines are a result of Shou-Yu Liang's extensive background in practicing and coaching Wushu. In this series, Shou-Yu Liang focuses on one particular approach in each routine. The shuaijiao routine focuses on take down techniques, the qinna routine focuses on grappling techniques, the quan routine focuses on arm strikes, the zhang routine focuses on palm attacks, and the tui routine focuses on kicking techniques. Learning these routines will allow you to gain a greater insight into the extensive and broad content of Wushu and assist you in becoming a well-rounded martial artist. It is our hope that you will benefit from Shou-Yu Liang's extensive experience and waste no time in attaining greater heights in Wushu.

The content of this book focuses on 36 practical take down techniques that flows from one technique into the next. We have photographs of the routine on the top of the pages. Below each of the photographs of the routine are photographs of the actual applications of each move. As you learn the routine you will be able to see the practical application of each movement. Try to learn the routine first. Once you have memorized the routine, then visualize engaging an opponent as you practice each move. To make the movements more realistic, you will need to practice with a partner. Alternate with your partner. One of you can be the attacker, the other can be the defender. Common sense is essential to prevent unnecessary injuries during your training.

At the end of this book is a glossary of some terms that are used in this book. This is included to give you a better understanding of these terms.

無 極 逍 遙 摔

引 言

　　所有的傳統武術門派都有他們各自的武術套路。套路中包括著各門派的訓練重點。如長拳套路中注重腿法。南拳套路中注重拳法和橋法。而內家拳則注重以柔克剛，引進落空。在各種套路中踢法和打法都很明顯。在很多套路中也包括不少的摔法和拿法。

　　摔跤沒有固定的套路。但大多數的武術門派中都有一定的摔法。摔跤在古時後就已經是一種競賽活動。以前，摔跤也叫角抵，角力，相撲等。在武術的散手搏擊中也常使用快摔之法而取勝對手。

　　散手快摔和傳統的摔跤競賽不同。散手快摔不和對手扭抱一團。而是一碰就摔，在一踢或一打之後有機會就摔。利用巧勁，脆勁，反關節及人體的杠杆作用跌倒對手。常常只是一轉腰，一抖肩，一勾腿就將對手跌倒。

　　從古到今，有效的，合符道理的武術技擊方法都早已被前人創造。但武術仍然在不斷進步和發展。新的一代在學習和繼承前輩的經驗的基礎上，加上自己的心得體會，仍然在不斷的創新。在武術的訓練方法上，實際運用和演練的風格方面，在如何訓練學生，讓學生更快的全面的理解武術技術和知識方面都還有待進步。

　　梁守渝先生是當今武術界最富豐富經驗的武術家之一。從六歲起，五十多年來從沒停止練功，不斷的學習和探索。他的座右銘是："活到老，學到老，練到老"。他廣納百家技擊術的精華加上他50多年的經驗和對武術很深的造詣。他在前人的基礎上新編了最適用也容易爲學者理解和記憶的摔法，拿法，踢法，拳法和掌法各一套拳術套路。學者能在這幾套拳里獲益，得到梁守渝先生超過半百年的經驗。不浪費任何時間就能接觸到全面高深的功夫。

　　這本《無極逍遙摔》是這套書中的第一本。我們希望能對讀者有所幫助。

無極逍遙捧

Wuji Xiaoyaoshuai Routine

Figure 1

1. Grab the Arm and Push the Knee
别，岩鹰展翅

Movements: Start with your feet together and arms next to your sides
　　　(Figure 1). Raise your left hand up in front of you, with your
　　　arm slightly bent and fingers pointing upward (Figure 2). Step
　　　to your back left corner with your left foot. At the same time,
　　　rotate your left palm out and pull to your left, and lift your right
　　　hand up slightly then push down (Figure 3).

Figure 2   Figure 3

Figure 2A   Figure 3A

Application: Opponent punches with his right fist to your head. You lift your left arm up to intercept his right punch (Figure 2A). Step in at an angle away from your opponent, while grabbing a hold of his right wrist and pulling to your left. At the same time, strike down with your right hand on his knee to take him down (Figure 3A).

Figure 4   Figure 5

Figure 4A   Figure 5A

2. EMBRACE THE WAIST AND PUSH THE CHIN
搓，抱腰搓顎

Movements: Step to your left with your right foot, while extending your
right arm up and forward (Figure 4). Take another step forward
with your left foot while extending your left arm over your right
arm and coiling forward and down (Figure 5). Shift your weight
forward to your left leg. At the same time, hook your left hand

Figure 6

Figure 6A

back, while pulling your right hand back from under your left arm, then pushing forward and up (Figure 6).

Application: Opponent punches with his right fist to your head. You extend your right arm forward to intercept (Figure 4A). Step forward with your left foot to the right of your opponent. At the same time, use your left arm to push his arm down while striking to his lower rib cage with your left palm (Figure 5A). Shift your weight forward and strike to his chest with your right palm, and hook his lower back with your left hand to take him down (Figure 6A).

23

3. Embrace Waist, Push the Chin, and Trip the Leg 绊，抱腰搓颔绊

Movements: Bring your right leg forward past your left foot (Figure 7). Kick back and down with your right foot while pushing in the opposite direction with your right palm (Figure 8).

Application: From the previous technique, if your opponent is able to prevent you from taking him down, strike up with your right palm to his chin (Figure 7A). Then bring your right leg behind his right leg and sweep back, while continuing to push with your right palm to take him down (Figure 8A).

Figure 7

Figure 8

Figure 7A

Figure 8A

Figure 9   Figure 10

Figure 9A   Figure 10A

4. PULL THE NECK AND PUSH THE KNEE
採，抹脖採按

Movements: Step forward with your right foot while circling both hands
to your right (Figure 9). Continue circling your right hand by
moving it over your left arm, while stepping forward with your
left foot and shifting your weight forward (Figures 10 and 11).
Shift your weight back to your right leg. At the same time, pull

Figure 11

Figure 12

Figure 11A

Figure 12A

back with your right hand and push down with your left hand (Figure 12).

Application: Opponent punches to your head with his right fist. You intercept with both hands by circling your hands clockwise to your right (Figure 9A). Shift your weight forward, while pushing his elbow down with your left hand and striking to his neck with the edge of your right palm (Figure 10A). Hook your right hand on the back of his neck and pull down. At the same time, push on his right knee with your left palm to take him down (Figures 11A and 12A)

Figure 13

Figure 13A

Figure 13B

5. CLAMP THE ARM AND PULL DOWN
夾，夾臂抹脖採按

Movements: Circle your left arm clockwise up and place your right hand
            on top of your left arm (Figure 13). Move your right foot back
            and pull your arms down towards your right leg (Figure 14).

Figure 14

Figure 14A

Application: From the previous technique, if your opponent is able to
prevent you from taking him down, circle your left arm up from
under his right arm. At the same time, strike to his face with
your right elbow. Then clamp both arms around his upper arm
and shoulder area (Figures 13A and 13B). Step back slightly with
your right foot and yank him down (Figure 14A).

6. Press on the Leg and Push the Chest
捌，别腿捌擠

Movements: Step to your left slightly with your left foot and turn your body to our left. At the same time, extend your right hand forward and up while extending your left hand forward and down (Figure 15).

Application: From the previous technique, if your opponent is able to prevent you from taking him down, push on his chest with your right hand, while striking down on his knee with your left hand (Figure 15B).

Figure 15

Figure 15A

Figure 15B

Figure 16   Figure 17

Figure 16A   Figure 17A

7. Brush the Eye Brow, Hook the Groin, and Sweep the Leg　殺，拍手抹眉勾襠反殺

Movements: Shift your weight back to your right foot then bring your
  left foot back in and out. At the same time, bring your right arm
  down and extend your left arm up (Figure 16). Shift your weight
  forward. At the same time, swing your right hand
  counterclockwise forward and bring your left hand back next to

Figure 18

Figure 18A

your right shoulder (Figure 17). Hook kick with your right foot. At the same time, pull your right hand down and extend your left hand up in the opposite direction (Figure 18). Sweep your right leg back and down. At the same time, swing your arms counterclockwise to your left (Figure 19).

Application: Opponent punches to your head with his right fist. You raise your left arm up to intercept (Figure 16A). Shift your weight forward to gain some distance, at the same time, swing your right hand towards his eyes, making him defend up (Figure 17A). Hook kick to the inside of his leg (Figure 18A). If your

33

Figure 19

Figure 19A

Figure 19B

opponent is able to move his leg to prevent from being kicked, you sweep your right leg back. At the same time, swing your right arm towards his neck to take him down (Figures 19A and 19B).

Figure 20

Figure 20A

8. LIFT THE LEG AND PUSH THE NECK
倒，倒口袋

Movements: Shift all your weight to your left leg, circle your right foot
toward your left foot then out. At the same time, lower your
right arm down and bring your left arm across to your right
(Figure 20). Take another step forward with your left foot. At
the same time, lower your left hand and swing your right hand
up and forward (Figure 21).

Figure 21

Figure 21A

Figure 21B

Application: Opponent punches to your head with his right fist. You yield back, adjust your right foot, and intercept the punch with your left arm (Figure 20A). Then step behind him with your left foot. At the same time, chop along his arm to his neck with your left palm and extend your right hand to the back of his right knee (Figure 21A). Push your left hand down and lift your right hand up to take him down (Figure 21B).

Figure 22   Figure 23

Figure 22A   Figure 23A

9. LIFT THE LEG AND PUSH FORWARD
提，提腿搬

Movements: Shift your weight back to your right leg and swing both
　　　　arms clockwise to your right (Figure 22). Shift your weight
　　　　forward to your left leg and continue the circular movement of
　　　　your arms by lowering your left arm and extending your right
　　　　arm (Figure 23). Step forward with your right foot and chop

37

Figure 24

Figure 24A

horizontally forward with your right palm, while hooking back with your left hand (Figure 24).

Application: Opponent punches to your head with his left fist. You yield back and intercept the punch with your right arm while striking to his head with your left hand to make him defend up (Figure 22A). Then step forward with your right foot and strike to his neck with your right palm. At the same time, hook your left hand behind his right knee (Figure 23A). Push forward with your right palm, while pulling back with your left hand to take him down (Figure 24A).

Figure 25

Figure 25A

10. Press the Knee and Push the Back
擠，按膝捌擠

Movements: Circle your right hand counterclockwise. Then push your palms in the opposite directions inward (Figure 25).

Application: From the previous technique, if your opponent is able prevent you from taking him down, move your right hand to his back and push down on his back. At the same time, press down on his left knee with your left hand to take him down (Figure 25A).

Figure 26

Figure 26A

11. Hook the Leg, Grab the Knee, and Lean Forward 靠，跘腿擠靠

Movements: Take an adjustment step forward with your right foot then follow up with your left foot. At the same time, lift your left arm up and push forward with your right forearm (Figure 26).

Application: From the previous technique, if your opponent is able to prevent you from taking him down, step forward with your right foot behind his right foot. At the same time, lift his left leg up with your left hand and strike to his chest with your right forearm to take him down (Figure 26A).

Figure 27

Figure 28

Figure 27A

Figure 28A

12. HOOK THE LEG AND GRAB THE CHEST
耙，上步耙拿（撿腿）

Movements: Step forward with your left foot and swing your arms counterclockwise to your left (Figure 27). Change your right hand into a fist and pull back. At the same time, hook kick forward with your right foot (Figure 28). Continue to hook your right foot up, while punching forward with your right fist (Figure 29).

41

Figure 29

Figure 29A

Application: Opponent punches to your head with his right fist. You intercept the punch with your left hand while striking forward with your right hand (Figure 27A). Strike down with your right palm and grab a hold of his shirt. At the same time, hook kick to his leg with your right foot (Figure 28A). Pull your right hand back, then punch forward, while continuing to hook his leg up to take him down (Figure 29A).

13. SWEEP THE LEG AND HOOK THE CHEST
跰，撿腿跰

Movements: Sweep your right leg back and down to your right. At the same time, pull your left hand to your left and hook your right arm to your left (Figure 30).

Figure 30

Figure 30A

Figure 30B

Application: From the previous technique, if your opponent is able to
move his leg to prevent you from taking him down, sweep your
right leg back behind his right leg. At the same time, pull his
right arm down with your left hand and hook your right fist
towards his chin to take him down (Figures 30A and 30B).

Figure 31

Figure 31A

14. DODGE TO THE SIDE AND STRIKE TO THE CHEST
撞，閃身靠撞

Movements: Bring your right foot back in toward to your left foot, then place it in front of your left foot. At the same time, lower your right arm and bring your left arm across to your right (Figure 31). Step forward with your right foot and shift your weight on it. At the same time, lower your left arm down and up, and swing both arms forward (Figure 32).

Figure 32

Figure 32A

Figure 32B

Application: Opponent kicks to your chest with his right leg. You yield
back and lower your right arm, and bring your left arm across to
intercept the kick (Figure 31A). Step forward with your right
leg and swing your right arm across his abdomen to take him
down (Figures 32A and 32B).

Figure 33

Figure 34

Figure 33A

Figure 34A

15. TURN BODY AND STRIKE SIDEWAYS
捌，旋身捌

Movements: Step forward with your left foot and raise your left arm up (Figure 33). Step forward with your right foot and turn your body 90 degrees to your left. At the same time, swing your arms around (Figure 34). Take another step backward with your left foot and turn your body 180 degrees around, while continuing to swing your arms around (Figure 35).

Figure 35

Figure 35A

Application: Opponent punches to your head with his right fist. You intercept the punch with your left arm (Figure 33A). Step in with your right foot and strike to the side of his chest with your right arm (Figure 34A). Continue your striking momentum and step back with your left foot. At the same time, pull his right arm down to take him down (Figure 35A).

Figure 36

Figure 37

Figure 36A

Figure 37A

16. GRAB THE LEG AND PUSH FORWARD
推，摟腿推按

Movements: Bring your right foot in, then step forward. At the same time, lower your right arm and bring your left arm across to your right (Figure 36). Take another step forward with your left foot. At the same time, lower both arms down then up, and push forward (Figures 37 and 38).

Figure 38

Figure 38A

Application: Opponent kicks sideways to your chest with his right leg. You intercept by yielding to your left and lowering your right arm and pushing with your left arm (Figure 36A). Circle your right arm up and lock his leg tight with both arms, and push forward to take him down (Figures 37A and 38A).

Figure 39

Figure 40

Figure 39A

Figure 40A

17. TURN BODY AND ROLL BACK
擺，旋身捋擺

Movements: Step to your left with your left foot. At the same time, lower your left arm and bring your right arm across to your left (Figure 39). Step forward with your right foot. At the same time, hook your left arm up and press in with your right forearm (Figure 40). Step back with your left foot and turn your body

Figure 41

Figure 41A

Figure 41B

180 degrees around, while pulling your left arm in and pushing your right arm out (Figure 41).

Application: Opponent kicks to your left side with his right leg. You intercept the kick with both arms (Figure 39A). Step in with your right foot. At the same time, hook your left arm up and strike to his thigh with your right forearm (Figure 40A). Take a step back with your left foot. At the same time, pull his leg in with your left arm and push out with your right arm to take him down (Figures 41A and 41B).

Figure 42

Figure 42A

18. LIFT THE LEG AND PUSH THE CHEST
按，十字防腿提按

Movements: Shift your weight back to your right leg and step to your
back left with your left foot. At the same time, lower your left
arm and bring your right arm across to your left (Figure 42).
Shift your weight back to your right leg and turn to your right.
At the same time, lift your left arm up and push forward then
down with your right hand (Figure 43).

Figure 43

Figure 43A

Figure 43B

Application: Opponent heel kicks to your chest with his left foot. You intercept the kick with your left arm down and right arm up (Figure 42A). Shift your weight forward and lift his leg up with your left arm. At the same time, strike and push forward with your right palm towards his chest (Figure 43A). Turn your body to your right, while continuing to lift his leg up and push down with your right palm to take him down (Figure 43B).

Figure 44

Figure 45

Figure 44A

Figure 45A

19. GRAB ONE LEG AND SWEEP THE OTHER LEG
踔，童子拜佛

Movements: Shift your weight back to your right leg, bring your left
   foot in, then step forward. At the same time, lower then raise
   your left arm up in front of you (Figure 44). Step forward with
   your right foot, while lifting your right arm up (Figure 45). Turn
   your body to your left, while stepping back with your left foot
   (Figure 46). Shift your weight to your left leg and sweep back

Figure 46

Figure 47

Figure 46A

Figure 47A

with your right leg. Clamp your hands together and complete your turn as you sweep your leg back (Figure 47).

Application: Opponent kicks sideways toward your head with his right foot. You raise your left arm up to intercept his kick (Figure 44A). Step forward with your right foot and lift his leg up with your right arm (Figure 45A). Step back with your left foot, then sweep your right foot back towards his standing leg. At the same time, pull his leg towards your left to take him down (Figures 46A and 47A).

Figure 48

Figure 49

Figure 48A

Figure 49A

20. PRESS THE KNEE AND PUSH THE HEAD
搮，跳轉身別搮

Movements: Lift your right foot up and turn 180 degrees around. At the
same time, swing your arms to your right (Figure 48). Step down
with your right foot, then step forward with your left foot. At
the same time, lower your arms down (Figure 49). Slide your
left foot forward, while pushing your right hand forward and
pushing your left hand down to your right (Figure 50).

Figure 50

Figure 50A

Application: Opponent punches to your chest with his right fist. You
        intercept his punch by circling both arms clockwise (Figure 48A).
        Shift your weight forward. At the same time, strike and push
        forward with your right palm to his face, and push down on his
        front knee with your left hand to take him down (Figures 49A
        and 50A).

21. HOOK THE LEG AND CHOP LEFT
勾，左勾跌

Movements: Step forward with your right foot while circling both arms to your right (Figure 51). Low hook kick forward with your left foot. At the same time, turn your body to your left and swing both arms to your left (Figure 52).

Application: Opponent punches to your chest with his right fist. You intercept his punch by circling both arms to your right (Figure 51A). Hook kick to the back of his front leg. At the same time, chop towards his neck with the edge of your left palm (Figure 52A).

Figure 51

Figure 52

Figure 51A

Figure 52A

Rt kick
Lt kick
    ⌐→ then
        over

22. HOOK THE LEG AND CHOP RIGHT
粘，右粘跌

Movements: Hook kick forward with your right foot. At the same time pull your right hand down and push your left hand forward (Figure 53A). Then step down with your right foot (Figure 54).

Application: Opponent punches to your head with his right fist. You intercept his punch with your right hand, grabbing a hold of his wrist and pulling. At the same time, push forward on his arm with your left palm, and hook kick to the side of his knee to take him down (Figures 53A and 54A).

Figure 53

Figure 54

Figure 53A

Figure 54A

Figure 55

Figure 55A

23. Spear Under the Arm and Turn (Right)
穿，右穿脇抱頸跌

Movements: Shift your weight back to your left leg and move your right
  foot back. At the same time, raise your left arm and lower your
  right (Figure 55). Move your right foot forward and turn your
  body to your left. At the same time, swing both arms to your left
  (Figure 56).

Figure 56

Figure 56A

Figure 56B

Application: Opponent punches to your head with his right fist. You
 yield back and intercept the punch with your left hand (Figure
 55A). Move your right foot behind his right leg and strike to his
 chest with your right arm (Figure 56A). Turn your body to your
 left as you straighten your right leg to push his leg back and
 take him down (Figure 56B).

Figure 57   Figure 58

Figure 57A   Figure 58A

24. Spear Under the Arm and Turn (Left)
穿，左穿脇抱頸跌

Movements: Bring your right foot back slightly while circling your right
arm counterclockwise (Figure 57). Turn your right foot out and
step forward with your left foot. At the same time, extend your
left arm forward (Figure 58). Turn your body 180 degrees to
your right, while swinging your arms around in the same
direction (Figure 59).

Figure 59

Figure 59A

Application: Opponent punches to your head with his left fist. You yield
back and intercept the punch with your right arm (Figure 57A).
Press on his arm with your right hand, while stepping with your
left foot to the side of his front leg. At the same time, strike to
his neck with your left arm (Figure 58A). Turn your body to
your right and push back with your left leg on the side of his
front leg. At the same time, swing your left arm around to take
him down (Figure 59A).

Figure 60

Figure 60A

25. SPEAR THE NECK AND TURN
切，穿頸靠切

Movements: Shift your weight back to your right leg and bring your left
foot back slightly. At the same time, circle your left arm clockwise
(Figure 60). Turn your left foot out and step forward with your
right leg and shift your weight on it. At the same time, swing
your arms around to your left (Figure 61).

66

Figure 61

Figure 61A

Figure 61B

Application: Opponent punches to your head with his right fist. You yield back and intercept with your left arm (Figure 60A). Push his arm down with your left arm and step behind his front leg with your right foot. At the same time, turn your body to your left and swing your right arm across his neck to take him down (Figure 61B).

67

Figure 62   Figure 63

Figure 62A   Figure 63A

26. PULL THE LEG
拉，拉腿跌

Movements: Turn to your left and take a small step forward with your
left foot. At the same time, lower then raise your left arm up
and begin extending your right arm forward (Figure 62). Bring
your right foot next to your left foot and bring your right hand
under your left hand (Figure 63). Step to your right with your

Figure 64

Figure 64A

right foot. At the same time, pull your hands down and to your right (Figure 64).

Application: Opponent side kicks to your head with his right foot. You lift your left arm up to intercept it (Figure 62A). Bring your right foot next to your left foot. At the same time, hook your right arm under his leg and clamp down with your left hand (Figure 63A). Step to your right with your right foot and pull his leg down to take him down (Figure 64A).

Figure 65

Figure 66

Figure 65A

Figure 66A

27. HORIZONTAL ELBOW STRIKE AND TAKE DOWN
肘，橫肘跌

Movements: Bring your left foot to your right in front of your right foot. At the same time, raise your left arm up (Figure 65). Step forward with your right foot and extend your right elbow towards your left hand (Figure 66). Slide your left foot behind your right foot and turn your body 90 degrees to your left. At the same time, pull your arms to your left (Figures 67 and 68).

70

Figure 67

Figure 68

Figure 67A

Figure 68A

Application: Opponent punches to your head with his right fist. You yield back and intercept with your left arm (Figure 65A). Step forward with your right foot. At the same time, punch with your right fist to his chin, then follow up with an elbow strike to his chin (Figure 66A). Slide your left foot back behind your right foot. At the same time, grab a hold of his right wrist and pull with your left hand, and press down on his chin with your right forearm as you turn your body to your left to take him down (Figures 67A and 68A).

Figure 69

Figure 70

Figure 69A

Figure 70A

28. GRAB THE CHEST AND SWEEP BACK
抓，抓胸插步跌

Movements: Turn your body 180 degrees around to your right and bring
your right foot back in slightly. At the same time, swing your
arms around to your right (Figures 69 and 70). Change your
hands to fists, step forward with your right foot, and double punch
forward (Figure 71). Bring your left foot to the right of your
right foot, then sweep your right leg back. At the same time,

72

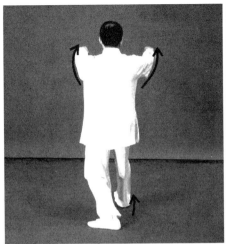

Figure 71

Figure 72

Figure 71A

Figure 72A

pull your fists towards your chest and turn your body around 180 degrees to your left (Figures 72 and 73).

Application: Opponent punches to your head with his right fist. You intercept his arm by swinging both arms to your right and pulling his arm to your right (Figures 69A and 70A). Let go of his arm and double punch to his head with both fists (Figure 71A). Grab a hold of his shirt, move your left foot behind your right foot, and sweep your right leg back into the back of his right leg. At

73

Figure 73

Figure 73A

the same time, turn your body 180 degrees around to take him down (Figures 72A and 73A).

Figure 74

Figure 75

Figure 74A

Figure 75A

29. GRAB THE WAIST AND OVER THE BACK THROW
揹，抱腰揹跌

Movements: Shift your weight back to your right leg. At the same time,
circle your left arm down then forward, and lower your right
arm (Figure 74). Step forward with your right foot and follow
up with your left foot. At the same time, turn your body 180
degrees around to your left and swing your arms around as you
turn (Figures 75 to 77).

Figure 76

Figure 77

Figure 76A

Figure 77A

Application: Opponent punches to your head with his right fist. You
intercept with your left arm (Figure 74A). Step forward with
your right foot and strike to his ribs with your right palm. Then
slide your right hand behind his back and grab a hold of his pants
(Figure 75A). Bring your left foot closer to him to anchor his
body on your hip (Figure 76A). Pull his right arm down with
your left hand, pull his pants up with your right hand, and push
back with your hip to take him down over your back (Figure
77A).

Figure 78

Figure 79

Figure 78A

Figure 79A

30. GRAB THE ARM AND OVER THE SHOULDER THROW
披，拉臂披

Movements: Step forward with your right foot. At the same time, circle
your right arm down then forward, and lower your left arm
(Figure 78). Take another step forward with your left foot and
turn your body around 180 degrees. At the same time, bring
your palms together over your shoulders (Figures 79 and 80).

77

Move your right foot sideways to your right and lower your body. At the same time, change your hands into fists and pull down (Figure 81).

Application: Opponent punches to your head with his left fist. You intercept with your right arm (Figure 78A). Lift his arm up with your right hand and step in with your left fist. At the same time, punch to his chest with your left arm, and continue your left arm movement up and grab a hold of his arm with both hands (Figure 79A). Slide your right foot back and push your hips into his body. At the same time, pull his arm down with both arms to take him down over your shoulder (Figures 80A and 81A).

Figure 80

Figure 81

Figure 80A

Figure 81A

Figure 82

Figure 83

Figure 82A

Figure 83A

31. LIFT THE BODY AND OVER THE SHOULDER THROW
挑，大挑襠

Movements: Lift your left arm up and extend your right hand forward. At the same time, step forward with your right foot (Figures 82 and 83). Shift your weight forward and stand up as you step behind your right leg with your left foot and turn your body around 180 degrees. At the same time, swing your arms vertically in the direction of your turn. As you turn, lower your body down again (Figure 84).

Figure 84

Figure 84A

Figure 84B

Application: Opponent punches to your head with his right fist. You intercept by raising your left arm (Figure 82A). Step forward with your right foot and strike to his groin with your right hand. Then continue your arm movement and hook your arm between his legs as you hit his ribs with your shoulder (Figure 83A). Shift your weight forward and lift him off the floor on your shoulder (Figure 84A). Step back with your left foot and turn your body around to drop him down (Figure 84B).

32. STRIKE THE CHEST AND SWEEP THE LEG
合，小得合

Movements: Step to your left with your left foot then bring your right foot next to your left foot. At the same time, swing your left arm across to your right and raise your right arm up (Figure 85). Lower your body and sweep back with your right foot. At the same time, swing your arms horizontally to your left (Figure 86).

Application: Opponent punches to your head with his right fist. You move to your left to avoid the punch. At the same time, swing your left arm across to move his arm to your right (Figure 85A). Lower your body as you sweep your right leg back into his right leg. At the same time, swing your right arm across his chest to take him down (Figure 86A).

Figure 85   Figure 86

Figure 85A   Figure 86A

Figure 87

Figure 88

Figure 87A

Figure 88A

33. PUNCH AND GRAB THE LEG WITH A FORWARD THROW 抱，沖拳抱腿

Movements: Move your left foot forward and bring your right foot back. At the same time, swing your left arm forward and lower your right arm (Figure 87). Take a small step forward with your right foot and punch forward with your right fist (Figure 88). Lower your body and scoop your arms forward (Figure 89). Push off

Figure 89

Figure 90

Figure 89A

Figure 90A

with your right leg and lift your arms up to your left as you stand up (Figure 90).

Application: Opponent punches to your head with his right fist. You intercept with your left arm (Figure 87A). Step forward with your right foot and punch to his head with your right fist to make him defend up (Figure 88A). Then drop down quickly, grab a hold of his front leg, and pull back and up to take him down (Figures 89A and 90A).

85

Figure 91

Figure 92

Figure 91A

Figure 92A

34. PUNCH AND GRAB THE LEG WITH A BACKWARD THROW 摔，冲拳抱摔

Movements: Step back slightly with your right foot and bring your left foot back slightly. At the same time, punch forward with your right fist (Figure 91). Move your right foot slightly to your right. At the same time, pull your right fist back then immediately punch forward again (Figure 92). Shift your weight to your right foot and punch forward with your left fist (Figure 93). Lower

Figure 93

Figure 94

Figure 93A

Figure 94A

your body quickly and scoop your arms forward (Figure 94). Push off of your left foot and lift your arms up and back (Figure 95).

Application: With your right foot forward, initiate a triple jab to your opponent's head, right jab twice and left jab once, to make him defend up (Figures 91A to 93A). Then drop down quickly, step forward to gain distance and grab a hold of his thighs with both arms. Lift him up and drop him over your shoulder (Figures 94A and 95A).

87

Figure 95

Figure 95A

Figure 95B

Figure 96

Figure 97

Figure 96A

Figure 97A

35. GRAB THE SHOULDER AND TRIP THE LEG
潑，潑腳

Movements: Step forward with your right foot and circle both arms to
your left (Figure 96). Step forward with your left foot and move
your arms to your right (Figure 97). Hook kick with your right
leg. At the same time, pull your right hand down and chop to
your right with your left palm (Figure 98).

Figure 98

Figure 98A

Figure 98B

Application: Opponent punches to your head with his right fist. You
    intercept with both hands to your left (Figure 96A). Step forward
    with your left foot. At the same time, chop both palms on his
    body and grab a hold of his shirt (Figure 97A). Hook kick to his
    front leg with your right leg. At the same time, pull down with
    your right hand and push to your right with your left hand to
    take him down (Figures 98A and 98A).

Figure 99   Figure 100

Figure 99A   Figure 100A

36. GRAB THE LEG AND OVER THE SHOULDER THROW
過，過橋大揹合掌收勢

Movements: Step back and down with your right foot and bring your
        arms down to your right (Figure 99). Bring your left foot next to
        your right foot and step forward, and lift your left arm up in
        front of your body (Figure 100). Step forward with your right
        foot and bring your hands next to each other (Figure 101). Turn
        your body 180 degrees around and move your left foot back

Figure 101

Figure 101A

slightly. At the same time, pull your hands forward in front of your chest (Figure 102). Bring your left foot next to your right foot and stand up completely. At the same time, lower both hands, then raise them up in a standard Wushu greeting, right hand fist and left hand palm (Figure 103).

Application: Opponent kicks to your head with his right leg. You yield back and raise your left arm to intercept (Figure 99A). Lift his leg up as you step forward with your right foot. At the same

Figure 102

Figure 102A

Figure 102B

time, hook your right arm under his leg (Figure 100A). Grab a hold of his leg and pull it over your shoulder (Figure 101A). Pull his leg down by bowing forward to take him down (Figures 102A and 102B).

93

Figure 103

Glossary

C

Changqun 長拳 Refers to Wushu styles that emphasize their kicking abilities and are capable of striking the opponent from a distance. It is characterized by rapid advancing and retreating movements.

China 中國 The nation located in the southeastern part of the Asian continent, with an area of ten million, four hundred, and sixty thousand square kilometers and a population of 1.2 billion people. It is an ethnically diverse nation with over fifty ethnic groups including the Han, Manchu, Mongol, Hui, and Tibetan.

Cultural Revolution 文化大革命 The period in Chinese history between 1966 and 1976. As the result of the struggle for power between the different factions of the government, every corner of the society was adversely affected. The damage done was especially apparent in the traditional cultures.

D

da 打 One of the four applications of Wushu for combat. It refers to the many shapes of the hand, as well as, the many defensive and offensive maneuvers of the hands and the arms.

Dapeng Qigong 大鵬氣功 A qigong training for health, as well as, for martial arts that develops incredible physical and energetic potential in the practitioners. It was passed down from the Emei Mountain area, and is one of Master Shou-Yu Liang's many areas of expertise. Grandmaster Liang learned this qigong from his grandfather beginning at age 6.

E

Emei Style 峨眉派 Refers to all the Wushu styles originating from the Emei Mountain area.

Emei Mountain 峨眉山 One of the well-known mountains in China, located in Sichuan Province. It is the highest mountain within Sichuan Province, with an elevation of 3,099 meters; well-known as a Buddhist, qigong, and martial arts center in China.

External Style 外家拳 A Wushu term that distinguishes the stylistic emphasis from Internal Styles.

F

Fan, Chiu-Mei 范秋妹 Master Wen-Ching Wu's mother.

I

Internal Style 内家拳 A Wushu term that distinguishes the stylistic emphasis from External Styles. Well-known Internal Styles include: Taijiquan, Xingyiquan, Baguazhang, and Liuhe Bafa.

International Wushu Sanshou Dao Association (IWSD) 國際武術散手道聯盟 An international organization that focuses on nourishing the well-rounded martial artist. Its training consists of six major components: free sparring techniques, take down and ground fighting techniques, Taiji Push Hands techniques, qinna and pressure point attack, internal energy (qigong) training, and martial arts routine training.

Its purpose is to function as a vehicle for members to learn new skills and to improve their martial arts ability. It is a bridge for martial artists all over the world to learn and share their knowledge, and to develop greater camaraderie between martial artists. The IWSD Association recognizes and encourages the uniqueness of various styles and traditions, but considers the cultivation of an individual's ability more important, than the distinction that divides one style or tradition from another. Their goal includes transcending the boundaries between styles to allow for the integration of a highly practical and versatile system of martial skill.

K

Kung Fu 功夫 Also romanized as Gongfu. It commonly refers to all styles of Chinese martial arts. The meaning, however, extends to an attainment gained through the input of time and energy in any discipline.

L

Liang, Helen 梁好 Master Shou-Yu Liang's eldest daughter.

Liang, Maria 梁爽 Master Shou-Yu Liang's second daughter.

Liang, Shou-Yu 梁守渝 The creator of Wuji Xiaoyaoshuai, and the coauthor of this book.

Liang, Xiang-Yong 梁向勇 Master Shou-Yu Liang's wife.

Liang, Zhi-Xiang 梁芷箱 Master Shou-Yu Liang's grandfather, an expert in Wushu and Dapeng Qigong.

Long Fist (*see* Changquan)

N

na 拿 One of the four applications of Wushu for combat. It is short for qinna. It literally means to seize and to capture. The objective of qinna is to control one section of the opponent's body to immobilize the entire body; or to neutralize and counter control the opponent. The proper application of qinna allows the practitioner to subdue their opponent without having to injure their opponent. It also provides the option to seriously injure their opponent when the situation requires such a measure.

Northern Style 北派 Refers to the External Styles of Chinese martial arts originating north of the Yangtze River in China.

Q

qigong 氣功 Refers to any set of breathing and energy circulation techniques that are capable of improving health, preventing illness, strengthening the body, and for spiritual development. Qigong training generally include four approaches: breathing, body positioning and movements, vocalization, and the mind.

qinna 擒拿(see *Na*)

R

Red Guards 紅衛兵 Refers to an organization by a privileged group of people during the Cultural Revolution. They were not restricted by law. The privileged people included descendents of laborers, middle and low income farmers, revolutionary soldiers, revolutionary leaders, and people that died for the revolution.

S

Shaolin 少林 1. Refers to the Shaolin Temple, a Buddhist monastery known for its martial arts and Buddhist teachings. 2. Refers to Shaolin Kung Fu, the martial arts that came from the Shaolin Temple.

shuai 摔 One of the four applications of Wushu for combat. It is short for shuaijiao, meaning take down.

Sichuan 四川 One of the Chinese provinces, located in the southeastern part of China. It is a classic valley surrounded by mountains.

Southern Style 南拳 Refers to the Wushu styles originating below the Yangzi River in China.

T

Taiji 太極 Also romanized as Tai Chi. 1. The grand ultimate; the term referring to the dynamic interaction of yin-yang. 2. The name of the yin-yang symbol.

Taijiquan 太極拳 1. An Internal Style Wushu characterized by a soft and subtle appearance, with its training philosophy based on the Yin-Yang Theory. 2. A self-healing exercise known and practiced for its healing and illness prevention potential.

Taiji Push Hands 太極推手 Refers to the component of Taijiquan training that develops a practitioner's sensitivity to an opponent's force, the ability to neutralize the force, and counterattack.

Taiwan 台灣 An island province of China. Located in the Southeast China Sea. It was also known as Formosa, meaning beautiful island.

ti 踢 One of the four applications of Wushu for combat. This application utilizes the leg's kicking ability in both offensive, as well as, defensive techniques. An offensive kick is any movement of the leg with the intent of distressing the opponent. A defensive technique is mostly used for deflecting or blocking the opponent's kicks. Kicks are either accomplished with one leg off the floor or both legs off the floor to kick.

W

Wang, Ju-Rong 王菊蓉 A highly respected and accomplished Chinese martial arts expert. She was born into a Wushu family. Began her Wushu and traumatology training at age 5 under the tutelage of her legendary father, Wang, Zi-Ping. She became the first women Wushu professor in Chinese history. She is also an expert in archery and has served as a judge in national archery competitions. After retiring in China, she immigrated to the U.S. She is one of the first Wushu professors from mainland China to spread Wushu in the U.S.

Wu, Cheng-De 吳誠德 A highly acclaimed Traditional Chinese Medical doctor and professor, and a highly respected and accomplished Chinese martial artist.

Wu, Wen-Ching 吳文慶 The coauthor of this book.

Wu, Yu-Kuang 吳餘光 Wen-Ching Wu's father.

Wuji 無極 1. The state one achieves when one becomes one with the Dao, the state after transcending the duality of yin-yang. 2. The original natural of the Dao.

Wushu 武術 The proper term for Chinese martial arts.

Wu, Denise Breiter 吳迪倪思 Editor of this book. Wen-Ching Wu's wife.

X

Xiaoyao 逍遙 Means to stroll along without a care in the world; to be carefree, and to be master of oneself.

Xiaoyaoshuai 逍遙摔 The name of the shuaijiao routine choreographed by Shou-Yu Liang.

About the Author:

Shou-Yu Liang

Shou-Yu Liang was born in 1943 in Sichuan, China. At age six, he began his training in qigong, under the tutelage of his renowned grandfather, the late Liang, Zhi-Xiang. He was taught esoteric qigong and the martial arts of the Emei Mountain region, including Emei Dapeng Qigong. At age eight, his grandfather also made special arrangements for him to begin training Emei Qigong and Wushu with other well-known masters of the time.

By the time he was twenty, Shou-Yu Liang had already received instruction from 10 of the most well-known legendary grandmasters of both Southern and Northern systems. His curiosity inspired him to learn more than one hundred sequences from many different styles. As he grew older, through and beyond his college years, his wide background in various martial arts helped form his present character, and led him to achieve a high level of martial arts and qigong skills. Some of the training he concentrated on included: the Emei Styles, Shaolin Long Fist, Praying Mantis, Chuojiao, Qinna, vital point striking, many weapons systems, and qigong methods.

Shou-Yu Liang received a university degree in biology and physiology in 1964 then taught high school in a remote village in China. This was part of his *reeducation* program enforced on him for being born in a bourgeois family, by the government during the political structure of the time. His dedication to his own training and helping others to excel didn't stop during the years he was in the remote village. He began to organize Wushu and wrestling teams to compete in provincial tournaments.

During the years of the Cultural Revolution, all forms of martial arts and qigong were suppressed. To avoid conflict with the Red Guards, Shou-Yu Liang left his teaching position and used this opportunity to tour various parts of the country. During his travels, he visited and studied with great masters in Wushu and qigong, and made many friends with people who shared his devotion. His mastery of qigong and martial arts, both technically and philosophically grew to new horizons.

Shou-Yu Liang went through numerous provinces and cities, visiting many renowned and revered places where Wushu and qigong originated, was developed, and refined. Among the many places he visited were Emei Mountain, Wudang Mountain, Hua Mountain, Qingcheng Mountain, Chen's Village in Henan, the Changzhou Territory in Hebei Province, Beijing, and Shanghai.

At the end of the Cultural Revolution, the Chinese government again began to support the martial arts and qigong. During the reorganization and categorizing of the existing martial arts, research projects were set up to seek out living masters and preserve their knowledge. It was at this time that the Sichuan government appointed Shou-Yu Liang as a coach for the city, the territory, and the province. Many of Shou-Yu Liang's students were among the top martial artists of China. In 1979, he received the title of *Coach of Excellence* since 1949, by the People's Republic of China.

With his wealth of knowledge, Shou-Yu Liang was inspired at an early age to compete in martial arts tournaments, in which he was many times a noted gold medalist. During his adolescence, Shou-Yu Liang won titles in Chinese wrestling (Shuaijiao), various other martial arts, and weight lifting. After the Cultural Revolution, despite his many official duties Shou-Yu Liang continued to participate actively in competitions both at the provincial and national level. Between 1974 and 1981, he won numerous medals, including four gold medals. His students also performed superbly both in national and provincial open tournaments, winning many medals. Many of these students are now professional Wushu coaches in colleges, in the armed forces, or have become movie stars. In 1979, Shou-Yu Liang received several appointments, including committee membership in the Sichuan Chapter of the Chinese National Wushu Committee and Coaches Committee.

In 1981, Shou-Yu Liang visited Seattle, Washington. This trip marked another new era in the course of his life. His ability immediately impressed Wushu devotees. The Wushu and Taiji Club of the Student Association, at the University of Washington, retained him as a Wushu Coach. At the same time, Shou-Yu Liang taught at the Taiji Association in Seattle. In the following year, Shou-Yu Liang went to Vancouver, Canada, and was appointed Taiji Coach by the Villa Cathy Care Home. During the same year, he was appointed Honorary Chairman and Head Coach by the North American Taiji Athletic Association. He also began to teach classes in the Physical Education Department at the University of British Columbia (UBC).

In 1984, Shou-Yu Liang was certified as a national First Class Ranking Judge by China. He was also appointed Chairperson and Wushu Coach by the University of British Columbia. In 1985, Shou-Yu Liang was elected coach of the First Canadian National Wushu Team, which was invited to participate in the 1985 World Wushu Invitational Competition that took place in Xian, China. The Canadian team took Third Place after competing against teams from 13 other countries.

The next year, Shou-Yu Liang was again elected coach of the Second Canadian National Wushu Team, that competed in the 1986 World Wushu Invitational Competition held in Tianjin, China. A total of 28 countries participated. This time, the Canadian team took Second Place which was only second to China. Shou-Yu Liang and the Canadian success story shocked the Chinese nation, and news of their outstanding accomplishment spread throughout China.

In 1994, Shou-Yu Liang led the North American Martial Arts Exhibition Team for a friendship performance tour to ten major cities in China. His team received a warm welcome by the people and government of China. While in China, the team also competed in the International Wushu Competition held in Shanghai. This competition was represented by 32 nations. Shou-Yu Liang's students received 42 gold medals. Canadian premier, Mr. Jean Chretien, also wrote a letter of encouragement to the team. Many Chinese television stations, radio stations, and newspapers spread the news of the Exhibition Team all over China.

Since the beginning of the 1960's, Shou-Yu Liang has personally taught over 10,000 students. Additionally, Shou-Yu Liang has touched the lives of tens of thousands of students in his affiliate schools and schools of students' students. His students have received hundreds of gold medals in national and international competitions. Many of his students are currently teaching all over the world.

Shou-Yu Liang continues to gain recognition in China and abroad. In the past few years, Shou-Yu Liang was selected as "The Instructor of the Year" by Inside Kung Fu Magazine, selected by the China Wushu Magazine in the "Biography of Today's Extraordinary Martial Artists". He has been awarded the "World's Top 100 Outstanding Martial Artists

Professional Award", "World's Greatest Contribution Award" and "World's Outstanding Accomplishment Award." He has also been selected to be included in the "Current List of Famous Martial Artists" and in the Chinese "Who's Who in the World". The chairman of the China Wushu Association wrote this about him, "Uses his martial arts to teach people, and uses his morals to inspire people."

Since the beginning of his advantageous martial arts life, he has been featured by scores of newspapers and magazines in China, Europe, the USA, and Canada; as well as, has been interviewed by many television stations in China, the USA, and Canada, including the recent interview by CNN.

Currently Shou-Yu Liang is the Advisor or Honorary Advisor of over 20 national and professional Wushu organizations in China, the United States, and Canada.

Shou-Yu Liang has written and produced several books and videotapes including, *Hsing Yi Chuan, Simplified Tai Chi Chuan with Applications, Baguazhang, Qigong Empowerment, Chinese Fast Wrestling for Fighting*, etc.

Shou-Yu Liang's popularity increases exponentially every year. It makes him sad to have to refuse invitations to give workshops or attend International and National Wushu competitions. He has to limit himself from traveling too often. The demand for him has become so great that it is taking him away from his commitment to his family, school, and students in Vancouver.

His focus is now on his family, friends, and students; and continuing the promotion of Wushu. As he was fortunate enough to learn from his teachers, he is now focusing it on his students, and writing books to preserve what he had the privilege to learn.

梁守渝簡介

1942 年出身中國重慶市。六歲開始跟隨爺爺梁芷箱先生學習大鵬氣功，鐵布衫功和峨嵋派武功。後又在爺爺的介紹下向十多位前輩老師學習少林派，峨嵋派其它多種功夫。猶愛散手。17歲開始學習太極拳，八卦掌，形意拳與武當派功夫和練習摔跤，太極推手等。

1960 年重慶市第29中畢業。學習優秀被政府保送進入西南民族學院生物系。

1960-1964 年參加成都體育學院武術訓練。被選爲成都市武術代表隊成員。任西南民族學院武術隊隊長兼教練。參加各級武術比賽，摔跤比賽和舉重比賽。獲得多次第一名和前幾名好成績。開始學習佛家密宗修煉氣功。

1965 年由於家庭出身不好，被分配到山峽地區雲陽縣。參加一年社會主義教育運動後被分配到高陽中學教書。

1966 年開始文化大革命運動。四處流浪，遍尋名師武友學習各種武術。

1974 年中國恢復武術，被政府調到體育運動委員會當專職武術教練。任第一任雲陽縣武術教練。

1975 年任第一任萬州地區武術教練。又開始參加四川省和全中國的武術比賽和表演，獲得多次金牌，也在全國比賽中作裁判員。

1978 年被評選爲四川省優秀教練員，先進工作者，獲獎。

1979 年被評選爲全國優秀教練員，獲獎。被指定爲第一屆全國武術協會四川省協會委員，和教練委員會委員。

1981 年任美國華盛頓大學武術俱樂部教練。

1982 年任加拿大溫哥華市華宮太極和氣功教師。溫哥華北美太極聯誼會名譽主席兼教練。

1984 年任加拿大哥倫比亞大學體育學院正式教師，後任武術專業主任直到現在（1999）。是第一個進入美，加大學中正式編制的中國武術教師。

1985 年被選爲第一任加拿大國家武術隊總教練，到中國參賽，加拿大隊總分第三。

1986 年再作加拿大國家武術隊教練到天津參加國際武術邀請賽，加拿大總分僅次中國獲第二。

1987 年成立加拿大 SYL 武術學院，任院長，旗下有十多名教練員。

1988 年和加拿大，美國，蘇聯，中國的同道一起創建國際武術散手道聯盟，任第一任主席。目的是在各國推行以中國武術爲基礎的，培養全面武術人材的計劃。

1994 年任北美洲綜合武術代表團團長，訪問表演中國十大城市，得到加拿大總理支持並題詞。在中國時受到中國政府和觀眾熱情接待和歡迎。

1995 年被美國雜誌（Inside Kung Fu）選爲當年國際最佳教練員（Instructor of the Year）。

1996 年被中國百花洲文藝社出版的《中華武林著名人物傳》選爲傳主之一。1998 年 9 月在中國正式出版。

1996 年中國全國武術協會主席張耀庭先生題詞："守渝先生，以技教人，以德感人"。

1997 年第六屆世界杯，被選爲："世界傑出百名武術名人金牌獎"。

1998 年被全美武術協會（USAWKF）選爲國際三名最優秀武術大師之一（Outstanding Master）。

1998 年被選入《中國當代武林名人志》。

1999 年第七 屆世界杯，被選爲："世界最佳武術貢獻金牌獎"和"世界傑出武術成就獎"。

1999 年被選入《世界名人錄》。（由香港世界文化藝術研究中心，世界人物出版社，中國國際交流出版社正式出版）

1995-1999 在加拿大，美國全國性武術比賽，泛美洲武術
比賽和多次國際武術比賽中作仲裁，副總裁判長和
總裁判長。

1999 再次被選為加拿大國家武術隊教練參加在香港舉辦
的武術錦標賽。

其它任職和名譽任職：

加拿大國際總會副會長

加拿大聯合武術協會名譽主席，名譽總教練

加拿大武術團體聯合總會顧問

美國全國武術協會（USAWKF）顧問。

美國全國氣功學會顧問

美國全國氣功協會理事

世界武術歷史學會第一任名譽主席

中國四川省武協委員

中國重慶市武協顧問

中國黑龍江省武術館名譽館長

中國上海市硬氣功功法研究會顧問

中國《防身與制敵》雜誌顧問

中國三峽易經研究學會名譽主席

曾被中國，美國，加拿大，歐州，日本，幾十份報刊
雜誌介紹，包括中國的《人民日報》。被七份國內
外雜誌選為封面人物。幾十次被中國，加拿大，美
國，英國，墨西哥等電視節目報道，多次接受中國
，美國，加拿大國家電視台專訪，包括 CNN 世界廣
播電台。

由於參與社會活動和在社會上的知名度，曾會見加拿
大總理 Jean Chretien。八十年代會見過中國總理趙紫
陽，也榮幸代表華人會見中國國家主席江澤民先生
⋯近四十年來，梁守渝在中國，美國，加拿大和歐
洲各大城市親自教授過的學生（包括公開課，講座
等）有數萬人之多。如包括學生的學生，那就更多
了。訓練的運動員中，獲得全國性和個種國際比賽
的金牌數已超過一百多塊。很多學生已經成為有名
的武術大師，氣功大師，武術專職教練員，軍隊和
警察中的武術教官，功夫演員，大學的教授講師等
。有十幾位學生都被選入了《中國當代武林名人志》。

出版過的書籍有：

八卦掌理論及運用

形意拳理論及實用

24，48 式太極拳理論及實用

散手快摔

氣功能

教學錄影帶：

八卦掌三卷

形意拳三卷

24 式太極拳一卷

24 式太極拳及其運用（包括 48 式太極拳套）

孫式太極拳及其運用一卷

吳式太極拳及其運用一卷

32 式太極劍一卷

無極逍遙摔一卷

醫療健康氣功一卷

小周天功法一卷

密宗九節佛風一卷

About the Author:

Wen-Ching Wu

Wen-Ching Wu was born in Taiwan, China in 1964. He loved Wushu and other sports since a young age. Like all other youngsters his age, he dabbled in Southern Wushu with his family and relatives. During high school he was on the school's basketball and softball teams. He graduated from high school as a salutatorian. He came to the U.S. in 1983 to study Mechanical Engineering. In 1988, he graduated with honors from Northeastern University, with a BSME degree.

Wen-Ching Wu is the son of Mr. and Mrs. Yu-Kuang Wu. With the support of his parents, Wen-Ching Wu was given an incredible opportunity to experience the world—from Asia to Africa, to North America... He is the protege of Shou-Yu Liang. With the guidance of Shou-Yu Liang, Wen-Ching Wu has excelled in both the Internal Styles, External Styles, and qigong. Wen-Ching Wu is the adopted son of Professor Ju-Rong Wang and Dr. Cheng-De Wu. With their guidance, Wen-Ching Wu has also excelled in Chaquan, Taijiquan, and qigong.

Wen-Ching Wu reached a martial arts highlight in 1990 when he competed in the United States National Chinese Martial Arts Competition where he was awarded the Grand Champion award in both Internal and External Styles. He competed in 8 events in 1990 and was ranked first in every event he competed in.

Since then, he has been focusing his efforts on teaching and writing. In 1991, he and his wife, Denise, founded The Way of the Dragon, Ltd. He then began teaching and writing full time, and traveling to other states and countries to offer seminars. Below are some of Wen-Ching Wu's accomplishments and appointments:

1993—Published *A Guide to Taijiquan* book.

1994—Published the *Baguazhang* book.

1995—Published *A Complete Tai Chi Chuan Workout Tape* and *Qi Permeating Technique Audio Tape*

1997—Awarded Master Level II Instructor by the International Wushu Sanshou Dao Association (IWSD).

1997—Published the *Qigong Empowerment* book, *Health Maintenance qigong* video, *Microcosmic Circulation Qigong* video, and *Nine Segment Buddhist Breathing Qigong* video.

1998—Awarded three Outstanding Performance awards at the Fourth Shanghai International Wushu Festival/Competition

1998—Published *Feel the Qi* video, *Tai Chi Beginning Workout Partner* video, and *Tai Chi Beginning* book.

1998—Selected to be included in the "Current List of China's Wushu Masters"

1999—Appointed as a United States of America Wushu-Kung Fu Federation (USAWKF) Advisor

1991-1999—Served as a judge in the U.S. National and International Wushu competitions.

Wen-Ching Wu has been giving workshops in Internal Style, External Style, and Qigong throughout the U.S. and Europe. His workshops have been very well received by participants. He has been featured in several TV programs in the U.S. To date, he has written or coauthored over 10 books and videos. Currently, he is working on several other books about Chinese martial arts and qigong, to be published by The Way of the Dragon Publishing in the near future.

吳 文 慶 簡 介

吳 文 慶 出 身 中 國 台 灣 省。從 小 就 熱 愛 武 術 和 其 它 體 育 運 動。小 學 時 隨 家 長 練 過 南 拳。高 中 時 代 表 學 校 棒 球 隊 和 籃 球 隊。從 師 梁 守 渝 大 師 學 習 峨 嵋，少 林，武 當 派 武 術，摔 跤，和 氣 功 修 煉。是 梁 師 在 美 國 的 得 意 大 弟 子。他 也 從 師 王 菊 蓉 教 授 和 吳 誠 德 教 授 學 習 查 拳，太 極，和 氣 功。是 王 老 和 吳 老 的 義 子。以 下 是 吳 文 慶 的 一 些 簡 歷。

1964 年 出 身 台 灣 省。父 親 吳 餘 光。母 親 范 秋 妹。祖 先 從 廣 東 梅 縣 移 民 台 灣。

1983 以 優 秀 的 成 績 高 中 畢 業。畢 業 後 進 美 國 東 北 大 學 機 械 工 程 系。

1988 年 以 優 秀 的 成 績 畢 業 於 美 國 東 北 大 學 機 械 工 程 系 獲 學 士 學 位。

1990 年 在 休 士 頓 的 全 美 武 術 大 賽 中 獲 得 八 項 金 牌。奪 得 內 家 拳 術，外 家 拳 術 兩 項 總 冠 軍 威 震 賽 場。

1991 年 成 立 美 國 龍 道 健 全 武 學 院，任 院 長。同 時 也 在 美 國 麻 州 大 學 任 武 術，太 極 和 氣 功 教 師。

1993 年 出 版 了《24，48 式 太 極 拳 理 論 及 實 用》。

1994 年 出 版 了《八 卦 掌 理 論 及 運 用》。

1995 年 出 版 了 一 卷 太 極 拳 教 學 錄 影 帶 和 一 卷 貫 氣 法 錄 音 帶。

1997 年 出 版 了《氣 功 能》和 三 卷 氣 功 教 學 錄 影 帶。

1997 年 任 職 國 際 武 術 散 手 道 聯 盟 行 政 辦 公 室 主 任，美 國 羅 德 島 主 席，和 大 師 級 教 練。

1998 年 參 加 第 四 屆 國 際 博 覽 會 比 賽 表 演 三 項 都 得 到 特 別 優 秀 獎。獲 得 金 牌。

1998 年 被 選 入《中 國 當 代 武 林 名 人 志》。

1999 年 被 聘 爲 全 美 武 術 協 會 (USAWKF) 顧 問。

1991-1999 在 美 國 和 國 際 武 術 比 賽 中 作 裁 判 員。

吳文慶對內家和外家拳術都有很高的照詣。他全面的學習各門各派的武術，包括少林派，峨嵋派與武當派多種功夫。對武術的踢打摔拿和多種武器都有很高的功力。練拳時能剛能柔，虛實分明。發勁時眼到手到力道十足。做到意動身隨形意並重充分的表現出武術的精，氣，神。對道家佛家醫療和武術氣功也有很深的研究。

他經常在北美和歐洲各地演講傳授武術和氣功受到學生們的愛戴。他也多次接受美國電視台的採訪報道。1993年到今他著有十多種武術，氣功書籍和教學錄影帶深受各地讀者歡迎。

Bibliography

1. Liang, Shou-Yu & Wu, Wen-Ching. *Qigong Empowerment.* East Providence, RI: The Way of the Dragon Publishing, 1997.

2. Wu, Wen-Ching. *Tai Chi Beginning.* East Providence, RI: The Way of the Dragon Publishing, 1998.

Index

The Way of the Dragon Publishing
Product Descriptions

Xiaoyaoshuai (video)

By Shou-Yui Liang & Wen-Ching Wu
ISBN 1-889659-18-5   60 Minutes

This is the video companion for the *Xiaoyaoshuai* book. It is demonstrated by Shou-Yu Liang with a voice over by Wen-Ching Wu. This video presents the Xiaoyaoshuai routine in small sections, followed by a demonstration of each take down technique presented in the book.

Qigong Empowerment — A Guide to Medical, Taoist, Buddhist, and Wushu Energy Cultivation

By Shou-Yu Liang & Wen-Ching Wu
ISBN 1-889659-02-9   7 X 10 Paperback   348 Pgs

Qigong Empowerment is the most unique and complete volume ever written in the English language on Qigong (Chi Kung), the attainment of energy. It is a volume that you can refer to over and over again for all your energy studies. This book includes all the major energy training schools in ancient China:

- Medical Qigong theories and training methods to strengthen the organs and to rejuvenate overall health.
- Taoist Qigong cultivation and training outline, from the basic to the most profound methods, to foster Essence, Qi, and Spirit.
- Buddhist Qigong empowering methods to develop the Esoteric Abilities of the Body, Speech, and Mind.
- Emitting, Absorbing, and Healing Qigong to develop your healing ability.
- Wushu (martial arts) Iron Shirt, Iron Palm, Iron Fist Qigong for developing your ultimate physical potential.

Qi Permeating Technique

By Wen-Ching Wu
ISBN 1-889659-00-2 22 Minutes

- This is a voice guided qigong imagery exercise. It is an effective method to achieve a harmonious relationship between mind, body, and qi.
- It trains your mind to absorb the *pure essence* of the universe into your body through your *baihui* and to drain out the impurities through your feet.

Health Maintenance Qigong

By Shou-Yu Liang & Wen-Ching Wu
ISBN 1-889659-06-1 60 Minutes

- Health Maintenance Qigong is done to balance the energy in the vital organs. This qigong can be used for attaining better health and for healing organ related illnesses.

- Includes the vital organ qigong methods for the: Lungs, Kidneys, Liver, Heart, Stomach, Spleen, and Triple Burner; along with the 6 Healing Sounds.

- Designed both as a learning reference and as a guided qigong workout partner.

Microcosmic Circulation Qigong

By Shou-Yu Liang & Wen-Ching Wu
ISBN 1-889659-09-6 80 Minutes

- Microcosmic Circulation was once a closely guarded and mystifying qigong method for Fostering Jing into Qi.

- It is an important and essential stage in Taoist energy cultivation for health, longevity, as well as, for spiritual development.

- This video is designed to assist you in completing the Microcosmic Circulation, and take your qigong attainment to the next level!

Nine Segment Buddhist Breathing Qigong

By Shou-Yu Liang & Wen-Ching Wu
ISBN 1-889659-11-8 50 Minutes

- Tantric Buddhist Qigong utilizes the Esoteric Abilities of the Body, Speech, and Mind to attain health, longevity, and for spiritual development.

- Nine Segment Buddhist Breathing Qigong combines the three esoterics by using body and hand seals, mantras, and visualization, to purify the body.

- This tape is designed to guide you through the breathing patterns to purify the Three Channels. When the Three Channels are open, the *dormant fire* of the Root Chakra can be awaken for greater health, as well as, spiritual realization.

Feel the Qi

By Wen-Ching Wu
ISBN 1-889659-08-8 40 Minutes

- This is an instructional and a beginner's guide to qigong. More than 90% of the people who have practiced the energy exercises presented in this video are able to feel their Qi after the first session!

- In less than 10 minutes you may also feel the magnetic sensation, warmth, and tingling, generated by your body. Allow yourself to experience this wonderful energetic phenomenon today!

Tai Chi Beginning Workout Partner

By Wen-Ching Wu
ISBN 1-889659-13-4   60 Minutes

- This is the video companion to the book, *Tai Chi Beginning*. It includes all the exercises described in the book, providing an excellent visual reference.

- It is also designed as a complete workout partner for an energizing workout at home.

Tai Chi Single Fan (book) — For Health and Martial Arts

By Helen Wu & Wen-Ching Wu
ISBN 1-889659-16-9   160 Pages

The *Tai Chi Single Fan* routine incorporates movements from the Chen, Yang, Wu, Wú and Sun styles of Tai Chi Chuan. It was created by Professor Wang, Ju-Rong; the first woman professor of Chinese martial arts. This routine combines the characteristics of Tai Chi Chuan with the artistic and martial functions of the fan. Practicing the *Tai Chi Single Fan* can help develop your flexibility, strength, balance, health, and further your Tai Chi training. Whether you practice Tai Chi as a martial art or for health and enjoyment, you will find Tai Chi Single Fan a wonderful addition to your overall Tai Chi regimen.

Tai Chi Single Fan (video) — Flying Rainbow Fan Series

By Helen Wu & Wen-Ching Wu
ISBN 1-889659-14-2   50 Minutes

This is the video companion for the *Tai Chi Single Fan* book. It is demonstrated by Helen Wu with a voice over by Wen-Ching Wu. This video presents the Tai Chi Single Fan routine in small sections. Each section is first presented with the front view follow by several repetitions of the back view. It is a valuable addition to the *Tai Chi Single Fan* book.

Tai Chi Sword (video) — 32 Posture Tai Chi Sword

By Shou-Yu Liang & Wen-Ching Wu
ISBN 1-889659-05-3   60 Minutes

The *Tai Chi Sword* routine is an important part of the overall training in the Tai Chi Chuan system. It has all the characteristics of the bare-hand routine, plus more. Tai Chi sword training adds depth and furthers a practitioner's Tai Chi Chuan training. The 32 Posture Tai Chi Sword routine in this video is a standardized routine. It is a beginner's weapon routine that works on the dynamic balance between the practitioner and the sword, and helps to improve the body's ability to work as a unit within itself and with the sword. This video is demonstrated by Shou-Yu Liang with a voice over by Wen-Ching Wu.

Price and Shipping Information

Xiaoyaoshuai (book)	*$18.00*
Xiaoyaoshuai (video)	*$48.00*
*Xiaoyaoshuai (book and video set *save $12.00)*	*$54.00*
Tai Chi Single Fan (video)	*$34.95*
Tai Chi Single Fan (book)	*$18.00*
*Tai Chi Single Fan (book and video set *save $4.95)*	*$48.00*
Tai Chi Sword (video)	*$34.95*
Qigong Empowerment (book)	*$34.95*
Health Maintenance Qigong (video)	*$39.95*
Microcosmic Circulation Qigong (video)	*$39.95*
Nine Segment Buddhist Breathing Qigong (video)	*$39.95*
Qi Permeating Technique (audio tape)	*$12.95*
*Qigong Empowerment (book, 3 video, 1 audio set *save $28.00)*	*$139.75*
Feel the Qi (video)	*$19.95*
Tai Chi Beginning (book)	*$14.95*
Tai Chi Beginning Workout Partner (video)	*$24.95*
*Tai Chi Beginning (book and video set *save $6.90)*	*$33.00*

Shipping & Handling (USPS)

Product Subtotal		*Add*
Up to	$19.99	$2.50
$20.00 to	$39.99	$4.00
$40.00 to	$59.99	$5.00
$60.00 to	$79.99	$6.00
$80.00 to	$119.99	$7.00
$120.00 to	$139.99	$8.00
$140.00 to	$169.99	$9.00

Add $1.00 more for each additional $20
over $169.95.

Order Form

Please refer to the previous pages for a description of the other exciting and informative products we offer.

The Way of the Dragon Publishing Order Form — xys

Qty	Item	Unit price	Total

Product subtotal		
RI resident add 7% tax to subtotal		
Add Shipping and Handling		
U.S. Priority Mail add $2.00		
Foreign Surface Mail add $3.00		
Grand Total		

I'm enclosing the Grand Total (❑ Check ❑ Money Order ❑ Visa ❑ M/C) payable and mail to: The Way of the Dragon Publishing
P.O. Box 14561
East Providence, RI 02914

Name:

Street: City:

State: Zip: Phone:

(Credit Card Order)

Card No.:

Expires: Signature: